SOONER THAN LATER

A Bible Study for the Terminally Ill

Maureen Sobolewski

ISBN 979-8-88751-804-6 (paperback)
ISBN 979-8-88751-805-3 (digital)

Christian Faith Publishing
832 Park Avenue
Meadville, PA 16335
www.christianfaithpublishing.com

Printed in the United States of America

To my husband, Brad
In you, I've discovered the love of a lifetime.
Thank you for our many adventures together.

To my sons and my daughters-in-law,
Bob and Lauren, Rick and Brittany
You will never outgrow my time and love; I'm still Mom.

To my grandchildren
Cora, Claire, MacKenzie, Everly, and Emmett
And grandbabies yet to arrive
You make my heart smile, forever.

CONTENTS

PREFACE

An occupational therapist is one of the medical providers often recommended for a terminally ill patient. I thought it odd; after all, my occupation is now "retired" or even "disabled." Yet I am happy I kept the appointment. My therapist emphasized energy, or the lack of it, as the focus of this stage of my life. She was spot-on with her guidance then, and even more so now, as my energy levels have begun to fluctuate. I filter my activities through this lens to assess whether or not the joy I can provide or the joy I might receive is worth the energy expended.

In writing this study, it is only natural that I have focused on ways to make this Bible study easy to use and energy efficient for the terminally ill person. Bible verses are not referenced with the expectation that the reader looks them up and writes them down, as is common in many Bible studies. In this study, Bible verses are recommended for further reflection in every chapter, but they are printed in their entirety, using the New International Version (NIV)[1]. Fonts are larger and easier to read. *Action steps* support a deepening personal relationship with Jesus while providing a path through this season of life. Finally, a music playlist is provided at the end of each chapter to engage the sense of hearing. These songs of praise, worship, joy, love, and hope are some of my personal favorites. On those days when reading and reflection are not physically possible, I pray that you can let the music wash over you and comfort you.

INTRODUCTION

I am dying. I had long ago accepted my struggle with rheumatoid arthritis (RA) and was prepared for a gradual loss of function. However, I was not prepared for the RA to affect my lungs, resulting in a terminal condition—constrictive bronchiolitis. It is a progressive illness that affects my ability to breathe. There is no cure, and there is limited treatment. My lifespan is expected to be between two and five years, and I am in year three.

Year one was spent in medical testing, trying to determine a diagnosis. Unfortunately, it was also the start of the COVID-19 pandemic, which meant delays in testing and treatment for myself and many others. Year two was spent figuring out a path forward; what do people do when they learn they have a terminal illness? My Christian faith propelled me to look for a Bible study for the terminally ill; certainly, there would be answers there. But much to my surprise, I could not find a Bible study for the terminally ill. Many books exist on the topic of death and dying. Many resources are also dedicated to caregivers of the terminally ill. Though I read many books and blogs and listened to sermons and podcasts, none of them fully met my needs.

I woke up one night with the words running through my head, "You need to write it." Immediately, I pushed the thought away. Why do I need to write it? I'm not a writer, and I don't even know if I have enough time left on this earth to write such a study. This happened on several nights, with the same response, and I thought I was simply stuck in a recurring dream. The last night this happened, I knew the message was from God. He told me He had asked me to write many years ago (true), and I refused (also true). Was I going to give Him the same answer this time? The sting of His rebuke hurt; as a Christian, I like to believe that I have continued to learn and grow in my faith and my relationship with Jesus Christ. My perspective changed from "why me?" to "why not me?" After all, I'm terminally ill and can offer the unique perspective I was searching for in a Bible study.

I have a small plaque on my desk containing a paraphrased verse from Esther 4:14, "Perhaps this is the moment for which you have been created." As I've encountered challenging moments throughout my life, I've always been inspired by this verse to step up to tasks and complete them. At this point, I now wonder if these past achievements were merely baby steps, leading me to this time and place to be obedient to God and to complete the task I believe He gave me.

Moses didn't think he could do the task set before him, yet he did, with God's help. So likewise, I knew God would guide me and help me write this Bible study. It is not dependent upon my ability, or lack thereof, but His willingness to work through me to accomplish the task He set before me. What an incredible honor; I am humbled and grateful for the purpose and meaning of this season. And so, I write.

CHAPTER ONE

Discovery

So do not fear, for I am with you; do not be dismayed,
for I am your God. I will strengthen you and help you;
I will uphold you with my righteous right hand.

—Isaiah 41:10

"You have an exceedingly rare illness for which we have no effective medical treatment." In my naiveté, I thought my doctor was telling me I would just have to live with my symptoms. Instead, she understood that I did not grasp the implications and said, "You are terminally ill."

Shock and disbelief are common reactions, and they were my first reactions as well. At first, there is a tendency to look outward, questioning the test results and the medical community and seeking a second opinion. When the prognosis has been validated, only then do we begin to look inward. We ask questions that cannot be answered, such as, "Why me?" and "Why now?" As Christians, we know our discipleship includes suffering, and we must have faith that God has a plan. Yet we are often surprised when it is our season to die.

God always hears prayers for healing; however, healing may not be God's will or His plan for your life. Matthew 26:39 tells us that Jesus, knowing His crucifixion was imminent, fell to the ground in the Garden of Gethsemane and prayed, "My Father, if it is possible, may this cup be taken from me. Yet not as I will, but as you will." The cup was not taken from Him, and Jesus suffered. We will suffer too. Romans 8:17 reminds us, "Now if we are children, then we are heirs—heirs of God and co-heirs with Christ if indeed we share in his sufferings in order that we may also share in his glory."

A terminal diagnosis is the death not only of our body but also of our relationships and future dreams and plans. An honest conversation with those you love, informing them of the illness and the prognosis, is necessary. Sharing the gifts you've been given, the gifts of time and knowledge, allows people to support you spiritually, physically, and emotionally. It is a time to ask and seek forgiveness, to love without limits, and to leave a legacy.

We are all terminal, but knowing it is a tremendous gift from God. We have been given the opportunity to filter out this world's many competing demands and focus on what matters— our relationships. Our relationship with Jesus Christ matters. Our relationships with family and friends matter.

It's time to pause our weeping. This season of life has many tasks to be done and lessons to be learned. But in the end, our testimony and our love are demonstrated not only in how we lived well but also in how we died well.

Reflections

In 1 Peter 5:10,

> And the God of all grace, who called you to his eternal glory in Christ, after you have suffered a little while, will himself restore you and make you strong, firm and steadfast.

In 1 Peter 4:1–2,

> Therefore, since Christ suffered in his body, arm yourselves also with the same attitude, because whoever suffers in the body is done with sin. As a result, they do not live the rest of their earthly lives for evil human desires, but rather for the will of God.

In 1 Peter 4:13,

> But rejoice inasmuch as you participate in the sufferings of Christ, so that you may be overjoyed when his glory is revealed.

In 2 Corinthians 12:9,

> But he said to me, "My grace is sufficient for you, for my power is made perfect in weakness." Therefore I will boast all the more gladly about my weaknesses, so that Christ's power may rest on me.

In Psalm 34:18,

> The Lord is close to the brokenhearted
> and saves those who are crushed in spirit.

Action steps

- Allow family members to notify friends and distant family about your illness. Sharing medical information on every call or conversation can be overwhelming. It intrudes on time better spent in happy reminiscing and moments of joy, love, peace, or comfort.
- Obtain a Bible, or download an online Bible, to use in this Bible study.
- Set up a Christian song playlist so that you can populate it with songs from this Bible study.

Playlist

"Oh, My Soul," Casting Crowns[2]
"Trust in You," Lauren Daigle[3]
"Cry Out to Jesus," Third Day[4]
"Need You Now," Plumb[5]

CHAPTER TWO

• • • ○ • • •

Surrender

Trust in the LORD with all your heart and lean not
on your own understanding; in all your ways submit
to him, and he will make your paths straight.

—Proverbs 3:5–6

Jesus was tested by the Pharisees, tempted by Satan in the wilderness, and cursed at and spit at by the crowd at the trial with Pontius Pilate. Jesus prayed for strength, and He prayed that His sacrifice, in the form of His crucifixion, would be lifted from Him by God. Although Jesus's prayer was not answered in the manner He was praying for, Jesus did not waver. He was obedient to God. Jesus relinquished His control over His life to God, fulfilling His plan for His life.

We fear times of testing. Intellectually, we know that testing can be a season of growth and that we will have matured in our faith and grown spiritually at the battle's conclusion. We know God's goodness and grace will abound on this challenging journey. We know God will use our struggles to offer hope and assurance to others. "And we know that in all things God works for the good of those who love him, who have been called

5

according to his purpose" (Romans 8:28). However, testing and trials are painful, and our human tendency is to avoid them. Yet testing and trials challenge the authenticity and sincerity of our faith so that shortcomings in our relationship with God are revealed and can be remedied.

Being terminally ill, we can no longer postpone this testing and must now make a decision. Will we spend our final days living in fear or living in faith?

To live in fear means living with worries and gradually losing control. Our thoughts are increasingly occupied by a sense of helplessness, concerns about being a burden, and fear of pain and suffering. We question whether or not we have fulfilled our purpose in life, often overlooking whether or not we have fulfilled God's purpose for our life. Although initially, fear is to be expected, we should not stay afraid as it deprives us of joy and energy. Christian author Max Lucado wrote, "The presence of fear does not mean you have no faith. Fear visits everyone. But make your fear a visitor and not a resident."[6]

To live in faith means to relinquish our pretense of control to God, to lean into Him and what He says is true, and to rely on every promise He has made. In Psalm 34:4, King David declares, "I sought the LORD, and he answered me; he delivered me from all my fears." The prophet Isaiah conveys God's promise to us, "For I am the LORD your God who takes hold of your right hand and says to you, Do not fear; I will help you" (Isaiah 41:13). Living in faith is surrendering your will and trusting God's will. Living in faith is resting in the assurance that God will direct your path. Living in faith is to acknowledge the power of God. He says, "Be still, and know that I am God; I will be exalted among the nations, I will be exalted in the earth" (Psalm 46:10).

As we face times of great trial and testing, I pray that we are more like Jesus, faithfully and obediently surrendering to God's will. God can be trusted. He has a perfect record, and if

He has said it, He has done it. In the case of future events, we have every reason to believe He will do it as prophesied. God promises He will never leave us or forsake us. He promises to love us unconditionally. He promises forgiveness for our sins. God promises He has a plan for our lives, unique to each of us. God promises to work all things for our good even during suffering. As believers, we have the assurance from God that if we trust Him to provide for our needs, if we live in faith, we will gain the peace needed to endure this season of life.

There is freedom and peace in surrendering our worries and anxieties to God and moving from fear to faith. We begin to live for today and let go of the future. We stop fighting death and using our limited time and energy to pursue medical miracles. We focus on the quality of time versus the quantity of time we have left. We focus on others instead of ourselves. We are learning to let go, to adjust our expectations, and to trust in the new life to come. "For none of us lives for ourselves alone, and none of us dies for ourselves alone. If we live, we live for the Lord; and if we die, we die for the Lord. So, whether we live or die, we belong to the Lord" (Romans 14:7–8).

Reflections

In James 1:2–4,

> Consider it pure joy, my brothers and sisters, whenever you face trials of many kinds, because you know that the testing of your faith produces perseverance. Let perseverance finish its work so that you may be mature and complete, not lacking anything.

In Joshua 1:5,

> No one will be able to stand against you all the days of your life. As I was with Moses, so I will be with you; I will never leave you nor forsake you.

In Psalm 26:2–3,

> Test me, LORD, and try me, examine my heart and my mind; for I have always been mindful of your unfailing love and have lived in reliance on your faithfulness.

In Hebrews 11:1,

> Now faith is confidence in what we hope for and assurance about what we do not see.

In Romans 15:13,

> May the God of hope fill you with all joy and peace as you trust in him, so that you may overflow with hope by the power of the Holy Spirit.

In Philippians 4:6–7,

> Do not be anxious about anything, but in every situation, by prayer and petition, with thanksgiving, present your requests to God. And the peace of God, which tran-

scends all understanding, will guard your hearts and your minds in Christ Jesus.

Action steps

- List all your fears and worries. Pray over them and then move them into God's hands for Him to manage.
- Seek a Christian counselor or support group if you need help with coping skills this season.

Playlist

"God Turn It Around," Jon Reddick[7]
"I Will Fear No More," The Afters[8]
"By Your Side," Tenth Avenue North[9]
"Out of My Hands," Jeremy Camp[10]
"Even If," MercyMe[11]

CHAPTER THREE

Spiritual and Emotional Self-Care

> Then, because so many people were coming and
> going that they did not even have a chance to eat,
> he said to them, "Come with me by yourselves
> to a quiet place and get some rest."
>
> —Mark 6:31

Spiritual self-care allows us to recenter ourselves and prepare our hearts for a deepening relationship with God as we enter this new phase of life. We reconcile our identity as a beloved child of God with the questions of why is this happening to us or why is this happening now. We pray about the decisions to be made. Spiritual self-care allows us the contemplation time necessary to develop a vision and a purpose for our remaining days.

Jesus frequently went away so He could be alone to pray for quiet reflection and to recover from the fatigue of preaching and working miracles. Mark 1:35 states, "Very early in the morning, while it was still dark, Jesus got up, left the house and went off to a solitary place, where he prayed." Similarly, in Luke 5:16, we find, "But Jesus often withdrew to lonely places and prayed." Jesus knew there was a time to be in the community and a time to be alone with God. Spiritual self-care provides us this time of quiet self-reflection, a time to sense and embrace the presence of God, and a time to store up spiritual reserves for the race ahead of us.

Emotional self-care is focused on the mind and body. We must learn to live in the present, living well for the day. Our bodies may be weary, and our health may be failing, but God is faithful even in the midst of our difficulties. Isaiah 40:29 reminds us, "He gives strength to the weary and increases the power of the weak." We trust God and His promise that He will provide for our physical needs. Our minds may be anxious, and we may feel discouraged, but we learn to quiet our minds, be still, and focus on God.

Paul wrote to the church at Philippi, "Finally, brothers and sisters, whatever is true, whatever is noble, whatever is right, whatever is pure, whatever is lovely, whatever is admirable—if anything is excellent or praiseworthy—think about such things" (Philippians 4:8). Spiritual and emotional self-care time provides clarity and spiritual growth. It is life-affirming and God-affirming. "You will keep in perfect peace those whose minds are steadfast, because they trust in you" (Isaiah 26:3).

Spiritual and emotional self-care activities can grow your relationship with Jesus Christ. Spiritual and emotional self-care activities often engage the senses, for example, praying on a nature walk, singing praise songs, and listening to music. Animal therapy, exercise, dance, or art therapy are additional options. Reflective activities include inspirational reading, listening to audiobooks, or journaling (organizing and capturing your thoughts on paper).

The first and greatest commandment is to love the Lord your God. To do that, we must spend time with Him, think about Him, praise Him, and tell Him we love Him. Spiritual and emotional self-care will help you establish a daily meeting time with God, deepen your relationship with God, and provide additional opportunities for prayer and praise. The stage of life compels us to spend more time building a relationship with God with a lesser focus on doing things for God.

Reflections

In Romans 12:12,

> Be joyful in hope, patient in affliction, faithful in prayer.

In John 9:2–3,

> His disciples asked him, "Rabbi, who sinned, this man or his parents, that he was born blind?"
>
> "Neither this man nor his parents sinned," said Jesus, "but this happened so that the works of God might be displayed in him."

In John 14:27,

> Peace I leave with you; my peace I give you. I do not give to you as the world gives. Do not let your hearts be troubled and do not be afraid.

Action steps

- Speak to a good listener and ask them to listen to your innermost thoughts and fears with a caring heart and an open mind.
- Create a spiritual bucket list.
- Set a time to mindfully listen to and communicate with God daily.
- Focus on what you can do and do not dwell on activities you can no longer do.

Playlist

"Breathe," Jonny Diaz[12]
"You Say," Lauren Daigle[13]
"The Words I Would Say," Sidewalk Prophets[14]
"Whom Shall I Fear?" Chris Tomlin[15]
"Great Is Thy Faithfulness," Carrie Underwood[16]

CHAPTER FOUR

Church and Pastoral Care

If one part suffers, every part suffers with it; if one
part is honored, every part rejoices with it.

—1 Corinthians 12:26

The church, as a body, often falls short in how it cares for its terminally ill congregants. Churches, after all, are comprised of people, and most people do not know what to do or how to behave toward the terminally ill. A collective fear of saying the wrong words results in not saying anything or, worse yet, not even acknowledging the ill person. People feel helpless, fearing they have nothing uplifting to offer. Sometimes, believing in God's power and ability to heal leads to fervent prayers for the person without recognizing that God may choose not to heal.

Pastoral care is equally challenging. Many Bible colleges and seminaries offer a cursory course on death and dying. Still, it is often insufficient in content and depth to be able to minister to the acutely or chronically ill congregant. Moreover, a new pastor may not yet have had meaningful or sufficient experience with death and dying to be comfortable with this aspect of ministry. Accordingly, our experience with chronic illness may be used by God to prepare and train church leaders and pastors. In 1 Peter 5:2, pastors are called to "be shepherds of God's flock that is under your care, watching over them—not because you must, but because you are willing, as God wants you to be; not pursuing dishonest gain, but eager to serve." However, the scope of ministry is great, and there is often insufficient time to tend to all the flock, despite a pastor's best intentions.

Those who are terminally ill have suffered a loss of purpose and identity. We are detached, watching others live everyday lives while ours has suddenly veered onto a new path. As Christians, we are comforted in knowing the end of life on earth is the start of our new life in heaven. It is the precious time between diagnosis and death that can be worrisome. In this season, we pray that our pain and suffering are meaningful and that God will use this time to change us and, in doing so, bring glory to Himself. This last measure of time is our final opportunity to develop a profound personal relationship with Jesus Christ.

How, then, can we integrate church and pastoral care to meet the needs of the terminally ill? The answer is found in Acts 20:35, "In everything I did, I showed you that by this kind of hard work we must help the weak, remembering the words the Lord Jesus himself said: 'It is more blessed to give than to receive.'" Acts of service communicate love, serve as a unifying force, and connect the church, the pastor, and the terminally ill congregants.

The apostle Paul was a prolific teacher, writing passionate letters to the young Christian churches to provide instruction, correction, and encouragement. In writing to the church in Ephesus, he said, "So Christ himself gave the apostles, the prophets, the evangelists, the pastors and teachers, to equip his people for works of service, so that the body of Christ may be built up" (Ephesians 4:11–12). Similarly, when Paul wrote to the church in Galatia, he wrote, "Therefore, as we have opportunity, let us do good to all people, especially to those who belong to the family of believers" (Galatians 6:10).

The pastor's role as the spiritual guide allows them to offer a Christian perspective about medical, moral, and ethical issues which may surface during this season. They have the opportunity to provide non-Christians with the hope and peace that a relationship with Jesus Christ will bring about. For the Christian, the pastor can offer guidance and answer questions that will enable a deeper spiritual relationship with Jesus Christ. Additionally, a pastor can pray over you and with you, listen to you and your family members, provide referrals to community resources, and provide fellowship and socialization.

The church's role is to ensure that the terminally ill person and their family feel loved and respected and remain active, cherished members of the church community. We can encourage the ill to share their life story and testimony, pray with them, read the Bible with them or to them, call them, eat a meal together, visit them and listen, sit in silence and cry with them, invite them to church activities and offer to drive, encourage Sunday School classes to create cards or artwork for them, and laugh with them. The church provides encouragement and compassion for both the terminally ill person and their family.

The Bible describes Jesus reaching out to the sick with compassion and tenderness: holding them, comforting them, and offering them forgiveness and healing. As Christians, the purpose of a church is not solely to teach and train us in our faith but to offer opportunities to work together as a community to serve one another in love, following Jesus's example. The scripture 1 Corinthians 12:27–28 reminds us, "Now you are the body of Christ, and each one of you is a part of it. And God has placed in the church first of all apostles, second prophets, third teachers, then miracles, then gifts of healing, of helping, of guidance, and of different kinds of tongues." God has equipped us to serve each other with compassion and love.

Reflections

In Acts 20:28,

> Keep watch over yourselves and all the flock of which the Holy Spirit has made you overseers. Be shepherds of the church of God, which he bought with his own blood.

In 1 Peter 4:10,

> Each of you should use whatever gift you have received to serve others, as faithful stewards of God's grace in its various forms.

In Hebrews 10:24–25,

> And let us consider how we may spur one another on toward love and good deeds, not giving up meeting together, as some are in the habit of doing, but encouraging one another—and all the more as you see the Day approaching.

In Romans 12:4–8,

> For just as each of us has one body with many members, and these members do not all have the same function, so in Christ

we, though many, form one body, and each member belongs to all the others. We have different gifts, according to the grace given to each of us. If your gift is prophesying, then prophesy in accordance with your faith; if it is serving, then serve; if it is teaching, then teach; if it is to encourage, then give encouragement; if it is giving, then give generously; if it is to lead, do it diligently; if it is to show mercy, do it cheerfully.

In Matthew 25:34–40,

Then the King will say to those on his right, "Come, you who are blessed by my Father; take your inheritance, the kingdom prepared for you since the creation of the world.

For I was hungry and you gave me something to eat, I was thirsty and you gave me something to drink, I was a stranger and you invited me in, I needed clothes and you clothed me, I was sick and you looked after me, I was in prison and you came to visit me."

Then the righteous will answer him, "Lord, when did we see you hungry and feed you, or thirsty and give you something to drink? When did we see you a stranger and invite you in, or needing clothes and clothe you? When did we see you sick or in prison and go to visit you?"

The King will reply, "Truly I tell you, whatever you did for one of the least of these brothers and sisters of mine, you did for me."

In Hebrews 13:17,

Have confidence in your leaders and submit to their authority, because they keep watch over you as those who must give an account. Do this so that their work will be a joy, not a burden, for that would be of no benefit to you.

Action steps

- Graciously shift from a giving mode into a receiving mode. Yes, it's challenging, but now is the time to allow church members to love and serve you.
- Share your life story and testimony at a service.
- Encourage church leaders to assess the buildings and grounds for inclusivity and ease of participation for all people, particularly those with chronic or terminal health conditions.

Playlist

"Hold Us Together," Matt Maher[17]
"Here I Am to Worship," Michael W. Smith[18]
"Lead You to the Cross," *No Other Name*[19]
"In Jesus Name (God of Possible)," Katy Nichole[20]

Spirit, Soul, and Body

May God himself, the God of peace, sanctify you through and through. May your whole spirit, soul and body be kept blameless at the coming of our Lord Jesus Christ.

—1 Thessalonians 5:23

As we near death, we seek a more profound knowledge and understanding of biblical details we once glossed over. We look for clarity in what happens to our body, our soul, and our spirit when we die. Unfortunately, the Bible does not clearly define these terms. Some verses seem to use the terms *soul* and *spirit* interchangeably, yet there are verses that seem to describe each term as a separate entity. Theologians, with great wisdom, struggle with the literal versus figurative translation and interpretation of the Hebrew and Greek words for *soul* and *spirit*. A detailed examination is beyond the scope of this Bible study.

In spite of this, we know that God exists as a Trinity: Father, Son, and Holy Spirit. Jesus himself said, "Therefore go and make disciples of all nations, baptizing them in the name of the Father and of the Son and of the Holy Spirit" (Matthew 28:19). Each has a different role, but they are one being. We also know, according to Genesis 1:27, "So God created mankind in his own image, in the image of God he created them; male and female he created them." Accordingly, for this study, we will adopt the perspective that we are tripartite, composed of a body, soul, and spirit.

We are to love and honor our bodies as they are God-given gifts. King David praises God in Psalm 139:13–14, "For you created my inmost being; you knit me together in my mother's womb. I praise you because I am fearfully and wonderfully made; your works are wonderful, I know that full well." Our bodies are our living, physical presence while on earth. The Bible describes how we are to care for our bodies: to nourish them (Ephesians 5:29), to train our bodies and exercise self-control (1 Corinthians 9:27), to offer them as a living sacrifice to God (Romans 12:1), and to honor them since our bodies are the temple for the Holy Spirit (1 Corinthians 6:19–20).

King David continues in Psalm 139:16, "Your eyes saw my unformed body; all the days ordained for me were written in your book before one of them came to be." You and I may be a little surprised that our days are coming to an end, but God is not surprised. It is the fulfillment of His plan for our lives.

Personality, desires, emotions, and thoughts all reside in our souls. We experience joy and sorrow, we praise God, we learn to love, we laugh, we cry, we develop attitudes and beliefs and values, we plan, and we solve problems. Our souls are the essence of who we are. Living with a terminal illness, we suffer through times when our body and soul are so tired and frayed that our focus becomes just surviving the next hour. Jesus knows this and encourages us, "Come to me, all you who are weary and burdened, and I will give you rest. Take my yoke upon you and learn from me, for I am gentle and humble in heart, and you will find rest for your souls" (Matthew 11:28–29).

All humans have a soul. Interestingly, the question is whether or not your soul is "turned on" or "turned off." If you believe that Jesus Christ is your Savior and live accordingly, then your soul is turned on by the power of the Holy Spirit. If you do not believe that Jesus Christ is your Savior, your soul stays turned off; you are separated from God. Free will abides in the soul.

In Genesis 2:7, we find that all humans have been given a spirit: "Then the LORD God formed a man from the dust of the ground and breathed into his nostrils the breath of life, and the man became a living being." While the Holy Spirit is strong and perfect, our spirits are weak, and we struggle with sinful temptations and heartache. The apostle Mark reminds us to "watch and pray so that you will not fall into temptation. The spirit is willing, but the flesh is weak" (Mark 14:38).

The moment we become believers and accept Jesus Christ as our Savior, the Holy Spirit and our spirit are joined. We are encouraged by God to follow Him as God said, "I will lead the blind by ways they have not known, along unfamiliar paths I will guide them; I will turn the darkness into light before them and make the rough places smooth. These are the things I will do; I will not forsake them" (Isaiah 42:16). Our spirit is nurtured by God's Holy Spirit to better comprehend spiritual matters, discover meaning and purpose, and align our spirit with God's Holy Spirit. Our relationship with God is strengthened; we can fully worship and praise Him as God had designed. Finally, our faith is acknowledged as "the Spirit himself testifies with our spirit that we are God's children" (Romans 8:16).

The tripartite view holds that all three parts of us, the body, soul, and spirit, were created by God. Our choices, our free will, impact the strength of each and the depth and intimacy of our relationship with God. God does not force us to enter a relationship with Him. However, if you choose to live apart from God while alive, realize that you have also decided to live apart from God after death. Free will governs what happens to us when we pass away. Our bodies die and turn to dust. Our spirits return to God. The Bible is quite clear about this, "and the dust returns to the ground it came from, and the spirit returns to God who gave it" (Ecclesiastes 12:7).

The soul of a believer goes to heaven to be with God for eternity. The soul of a nonbeliever goes to hell and is separated from God for eternity. As the Christian theologian Martin Luther has written, "Every man must do two things alone; he must do his own believing and his own dying."[21]

Reflections

In Hebrews 4:12,

> For the word of God is alive and active. Sharper than any double-edged sword, it penetrates even to dividing soul and spirit, joints and marrow; it judges the thoughts and attitudes of the heart.

In Job 33:4,

> The Spirit of God has made me; the breath of the Almighty gives me life.

In Luke 23:46,

> Jesus called out with a loud voice, "Father, into your hands I commit my spirit." When he had said this, he breathed his last.

In 1 Corinthians 2:12–14,

What we have received is not the spirit of the world, but the Spirit who is from God, so that we may understand what God has freely given us. This is what we speak, not in words taught us by human wisdom but in words taught by the Spirit, explaining spiritual realities with Spirit-taught words. The person without the Spirit does not accept the things that come from the Spirit of God but considers them foolishness, and cannot understand them because they are discerned only through the Spirit.

In 1 Peter 3:18,

For Christ also suffered once for sins, the righteous for the unrighteous, to bring you to God. He was put to death in the body but made alive in the Spirit.

In 1 Corinthians 15:50–55,

I declare to you, brothers and sisters, that flesh and blood cannot inherit the kingdom of God, nor does the perishable inherit the imperishable. Listen, I tell you a mystery: We will not all sleep, but we will all be changed—in a flash, in the twinkling of an eye, at the last trumpet. For the trumpet will sound, the dead will be raised imperishable, and we will be changed. For the perishable must clothe itself with the imperishable, and the mortal with immortality.

When the perishable has been clothed with the imperishable, and the mortal with immortality, then the saying that is written will come true:

"Death has been swallowed up in victory."

"Where, O death, is your victory? Where, O death, is your sting?"

In Philippians 3:20–21,

But our citizenship is in heaven. And we eagerly await a Savior from there, the Lord Jesus Christ, who, by the power that enables him to bring everything under his control, will transform our lowly bodies so that they will be like his glorious body.

Action steps

- Pray, so we may nurture our souls and spirits and develop a more intimate relationship with God.
- Grow in joy by giving more than you receive each day: affection, smiles, words of affirmation, small gifts, and acts of kindness.

Playlist

"Gracefully Broken," Matt Redman[22]
"Homesick," MercyMe[23]
"It Is Well with My Soul," Anthem Lights[24]
"Trust in Jesus," Third Day[25]

CHAPTER SIX

Dying Well

Blessed is the one who perseveres under trial because,
having stood the test, that person will receive the crown of
life that the Lord has promised to those who love him.

—James 1:12

In a sense, we are all terminal. Some of us just have forewarning. One hundred years ago, most people died quickly. Diseases struck the young and the old without warning.[26] We did not have the early diagnostic tools, medical treatment, or pharmaceuticals to fend off the infectious diseases that were the primary cause of death. Historically, we have moved from acute illnesses with rapid death to chronic, even terminal, conditions with advanced medical treatments that can result in many additional years of life. Even so, some pass after a short illness or, suddenly, without warning. But for many of us, we will enter into this *terminal* stage of life, where no cure is available, but there is a medical treatment to prolong life. For the first time in human history, we can anticipate our mortality.[27]

We can expect a continuum during this stage, which will vary significantly from day to day and person to person.

Living in past or future ↔ living in the present
Want to do activities ↔ need to do activities
Community-wide focus ↔ family/friend focus
Denial ↔ acceptance
Doing for God ↔ being with God
Why me? ↔ why not me?
Many priorities ↔ few priorities
Independent ↔ accepting help
Medical treatment ↔ medical comfort
Controlling tightly ↔ surrendering to God
Giving ↔ receiving

Our *normal* will shift regularly. We will grieve for our lost future. We will struggle with acceptance of our condition. Our physical energy will ebb and flow, sometimes daily, making the consistency of daily living nearly impossible. We will learn from our occupational therapists that we need to consider the energy cost and recovery of every activity we undertake. We will learn to navigate the world of durable medical equipment. We will complete mountains of legal paperwork. Our retirement and financial plans will be redone numerous times. We will make lifestyle changes before we are compelled to, such as downsizing or moving near family. Our mental and emotional health will suffer. We will cry over every real or perceived step down the terminal scale, as in the inability to complete a walk at the *normal* speed, opening a jar, or having to use a grab bar regularly. We withdraw, and our world becomes smaller.

Good news. Though the cares of this life are fading away, our spiritual life is about to undergo a renaissance, a rebirth. A terminal stage of life is a marvelous gift from God; it is a gift of time. This newfound awareness of time can foster a spiritually rich season of planning and growth. During this period, there is an opportunity to have deep, meaningful conversations with people as all pretenses tend to fade away.

You've spent your life modeling how you live to others, and now you have an opportunity to model dying. Your testimony carries significant weight during this season: refine it, and speak your truth to all who will listen. Forgive and be forgiven. Complete unfinished business. And finally, convey your heartfelt love and create good memories with your loved ones.

I want my husband, our children, and our grandchildren to know that I deeply loved them. I want them to feel it with all their senses and in all their memories so they can hold on to the simple truth that I loved them with all of my heart and soul.

As a Christian, it is not the final destination, heaven and eternity with God, which is scary. Instead, it is the thought of the journey to get there. Dying well is different for everyone; for me, it means I am surrounded by love, pain-free, lucid, and at peace. So what does dying well mean to you? And what actions will you take now to help you achieve your goals? Dying well is not just about managing physical symptoms; it requires thoughtful consideration and setting of emotional and spiritual goals and a plan to achieve them.

Jesus modeled the definitive lesson in acceptance for us in His final days.

> They went to a place called Gethsemane, and Jesus said to his disciples, "Sit here while I pray." He took Peter, James and John along with him, and he began to be deeply distressed and troubled. "My soul is overwhelmed with sorrow to the point of death," he said to them. "Stay here and keep watch."
>
> Going a little farther, he fell to the ground and prayed that if possible the hour might pass from him. "Abba, Father," he said, "everything is possible for you. Take this cup

from me. Yet not what I will, but what you will." (Mark 14:32–36)

Trust God that He will be with you and carry you through this spiritual journey. Remain faithful, trusting that dying is not the end but a transition into glory. Pray that He will use you, even now, to further the faith. Pray for a deeper personal relationship with God. Serve others with as much as you have for as long as possible.

As we travel this path, let us serve others, love our friends and families well, and deepen our love for and relationship with Jesus. Even as we live a good life, we prepare to die well.

Reflections

In John 5:24,

> Very truly I tell you, whoever hears my word and believes him who sent me has eternal life and will not be judged but has crossed over from death to life.

In 2 Corinthians 4:16–18,

> Therefore we do not lose heart. Though outwardly we are wasting away, yet inwardly we are being renewed day by day. For our light and momentary troubles are achieving for us an eternal glory that far outweighs them all. So we fix our eyes not on what is seen, but on what is unseen, since what is seen is temporary, but what is unseen is eternal.

In Deuteronomy 31:8,

> The Lord himself goes before you and will be with you; he will never leave you nor forsake you. Do not be afraid; do not be discouraged.

In Psalm 18:2,

> The Lord is my rock, my fortress and my deliverer; my God is my rock, in whom I take refuge, my shield and the horn of my salvation, my stronghold.

Action steps

- Create a memory box of objects that have touched your heart and then share the story behind each item with family members and friends when they visit.
- Write out your spiritual testimony and practice speaking your truth so that you can share it with others.

Playlist

"Who Am I?" Casting Crowns[28]
"In Christ Alone," Natalie Grant[29]
"Sovereign Over Us," Michael W. Smith[30]
"I Can Only Imagine," MercyMe[31]
"Fires," Jordan St. Cyr[32]

CHAPTER SEVEN

Freedom in Forgiveness

Be kind and compassionate to one another, forgiving
each other, just as in Christ God forgave you.

—Ephesians 4:32

Dr. Ira Byock, a palliative care doctor and author, proposes that four simple phrases will mend and nurture our relationships: Please forgive me, I forgive you, Thank you, and I love you.[33] As Christians, we know that there is another task to complete: asking God to forgive us. Forgiveness is not earned; it is offered to us as a gift. God grants this gift to each of us who requests it. The scripture 1 John 1:9 declares, "If we confess our sins, he is faithful and just and will forgive us our sins and purify us from all unrighteousness." We are forgiven and reconciled to a healthy relationship with God. In the same manner, we ask and offer forgiveness to others.

Why is it so difficult for us to both ask for forgiveness and grant forgiveness to others?

Although it may be challenging, we are to demonstrate humility and vulnerability and approach those whom we have wronged. The apostle Peter writes, "Humble yourselves, therefore, under God's mighty hand, that he may lift you up in due time" (1 Peter 5:6). When you ask people for forgiveness, you encourage restoration and healing, eventually bringing peace to both individuals. As a first step, we need to identify all those to whom we have caused suffering and pain. Next, we need to acknowledge the pain we've caused, admit our mistakes, and restore the relationship as best we can through actions and words. Finally, we must formally ask those we have wronged to forgive us.

Forgiveness may not be immediate; it is a process requiring time and effort. But working toward forgiveness allows those we've hurt to begin the healing process and to stop carrying the hurt and anger they have been bearing, perhaps for a long time. Being forgiven by the ones we've hurt allows us to let go of shame and guilt. Finally, as the Bible tells us, "And when you stand praying, if you hold anything against anyone, forgive them, so that your Father in heaven may forgive you your sins" (Mark 11:25).

Offering forgiveness to others is not excusing or condoning their behavior; instead, it acknowledges that people are imperfect and sinful and make mistakes. It is not easy to forgive when you have been deeply hurt. Sometimes, we will struggle to forgive those who haven't yet changed their behavior. Jesus taught us, "For if you forgive other people when they sin against you, your heavenly Father will also forgive you. But if you do not forgive others their sins, your Father will not forgive your sins" (Matthew 6:14–15).

To forgive is both an act of love and an act of obedience. Christ's sacrifice for the forgiveness of sins is more than sufficient to pay for our sins and those who have sinned against us.

Forgiveness is not earned by the person you are forgiving; instead, granting forgiveness is letting go of the need to seek revenge, keep score or punish, and diminish the hurt and anger we live with. We forgive others by faith, with an intentional decision, in obedience to God and His commandment to forgive. Forgiveness can lead to the reconciliation of relationships, provide closure for unfinished business, and provide grace and mercy for both the forgiver and the forgiven.

Forgiveness is an essential part of the Christian life; we forgive others as we have been forgiven. Forgiving ourselves is also necessary and allows us to be free to live as God intended, without guilt or shame. The need to keep score, replay hurtful events, and ask, "What if?" is eliminated. It is crucial to let go of sins we have committed if they have been settled with the power of forgiveness. They should not preoccupy our hearts or our minds. Time and emotional energy formerly used to nurse resentment and wounds can now be focused on the pursuit of love, leaving a legacy, and finishing the race strong in our remaining days.

Reflections

In Psalm 86:5,

> You, Lord, are forgiving and good,
> abounding in love to all who call to you.

In Colossians 3:13,

> Bear with each other and forgive one
> another if any of you has a grievance against
> someone. Forgive as the Lord forgave you.

In Ephesians 1:7,

> In him we have redemption through his
> blood, the forgiveness of sins, in accordance
> with the riches of God's grace.

In 2 Chronicles 7:14,

> If my people, who are called by my name, will humble themselves and pray and seek my face and turn from their wicked ways, then I will hear from heaven, and I will forgive their sin and will heal their land.

In Acts 3:19,

> Repent, then, and turn to God, so that your sins may be wiped out, that times of refreshing may come from the Lord.

In Psalm 32:1–5,

> Blessed is the one
> whose transgressions are forgiven,
> whose sins are covered.
> Blessed is the one
> whose sin the Lord does not count
> against them
> and in whose spirit is no deceit.
>
> When I kept silent,
> my bones wasted away
> through my groaning all day long.
> For day and night
> your hand was heavy on me;
> my strength was sapped
> as in the heat of summer.

> Then I acknowledged my sin to you
> and did not cover up my iniquity.
> I said, "I will confess
> my transgressions to the Lord."
> And you forgave
> the guilt of my sin.

In Philippians 3:13–14,

> Brothers and sisters, I do not consider myself yet to have taken hold of it. But one thing I do: Forgetting what is behind and straining toward what is ahead, I press on toward the goal to win the prize for which God has called me heavenward in Christ Jesus.

Action steps

- Ask God to forgive you.
- Forgive people who have wronged you.
- Ask people you have wronged to forgive you.
- Forgive yourself.

Playlist

"Forgiveness," Matthew West[34]
"Forgiven," David Crowder[35]
"Oh Happy Day," Gabriel Henrique[36]
"Forgiveness," TobyMac featuring Lecrae[37]

CHAPTER EIGHT

Pursuing Love

For God so loved the world that he gave his
one and only Son, that whoever believes in him
shall not perish but have eternal life.

—John 3:16

God created us to love. Jesus was asked, "Teacher, which is the greatest commandment in the Law?" Jesus replied: "Love the Lord your God with all your heart and with all your soul and with all your mind. This is the first and greatest commandment. And the second is like it: 'Love your neighbor as yourself'" (Matthew 22:36–39).

To love the Lord with all our hearts is a choice that requires action; it is not simply an affectionate feeling or a tender emotion. It is spending time with God, actively listening to His voice, praying to God, thanking God, and praising God; in short, it is cultivating a relationship with God. Your love for God is demonstrated by your obedience to God. "If you love me, keep my commands" (John 14:15). As we tell God we love Him, our relationship grows, and we are slowly transformed into the image of Christ.

To love the Lord our God with all our souls entails behavioral changes. We are to take up the cross and follow Him. In Mark 8:34, we find, "Then he called the crowd to him along with his disciples and said: 'Whoever wants to be my disciple must deny themselves and take up their cross and follow me.'" This is a serious commitment, requiring dedication. Following Jesus guarantees that our lifestyle choices will be affected. We must spend time with God. We must be willing to deny ourselves and cede control of our lives to God. We must learn to depend on God, praying to Him and asking for guidance throughout the day. Loving God with all our souls means we have learned to put Him first in our lives.

To love the Lord with all our minds is reasonably straightforward. We read, study, question, and contemplate the Bible. We may journal, create songs, or write a blog. We acknowledge how good He is to us and the blessings He has provided. For the terminally ill, understanding God's word and promises will provide knowledge and wisdom to endure and find joy and peace in this season of life.

God loves us unconditionally. He sent His only Son, Jesus Christ, to live with us and die for us. Jesus developed close, loving relationships with His disciples and sought to prepare them for His crucifixion and ascension into heaven. In John 13:1, we read, "It was just before the Passover Festival. Jesus knew that the hour had come for him to leave this world and go to the Father. Having loved his own who were in the world, he loved them to the end." Jesus revealed His love for His disciples even those He knew would desert Him or betray Him.

Jesus demonstrated His love for His mother, Mary, as well. While He was dying on the cross, Jesus saw Mary grieving for Him. Jesus also saw John, the only disciple who stayed throughout Jesus's crucifixion. In John 19:26–27, we learn that "when Jesus saw his mother there, and the disciple whom he loved standing nearby, he said to her, 'Woman, here is your son,' and to the disciple, 'Here is your mother.'" Accordingly, and in obedience, John took Mary into his own home and provided for her.

God created us to love others as He loves us. This is not worldly love, which says, "I love you because you love me." Instead, unconditional love says, "I love you, no matter what you've done or failed to do or what the future holds." It sets aside the love of self to love others well. Love is far more than a feeling; it is a deed. Love in action means encouraging others, providing acts of kindness and generosity, and actively listening to people to discern their needs. How well we love others reveals how well we love God. As the apostle John conveyed, "By this everyone will know that you are my disciples, if you love one another" (John 13:35).

Reflections

In 1 John 4:7–11,

> Dear friends, let us love one another, for love comes from God. Everyone who loves has been born of God and knows God. Whoever does not love does not know God, because God is love. This is how God showed his love among us: He sent his one and only Son into the world that we might live through him. This is love: not that we loved God, but that he loved us and sent his Son as an atoning sacrifice for our sins.
>
> Dear friends, since God so loved us, we also ought to love one another.

In Psalm 59:16,

> But I will sing of your strength, in the morning I will sing of your love; for you are my fortress, my refuge in times of trouble.

In 1 Corinthians 13:4–7,

> Love is patient, love is kind. It does not envy, it does not boast, it is not proud.
>
> It does not dishonor others, it is not self-seeking, it is not easily angered, it keeps no record of wrongs. Love does not delight in evil but rejoices with the truth.
>
> It always protects, always trusts, always hopes, always perseveres.

In 1 John 4:16,

> And so we know and rely on the love God has for us. God is love. Whoever lives in love lives in God, and God in them.

In Romans 8:38–39,

> For I am convinced that neither death nor life, neither angels nor demons, neither the present nor the future, nor any powers, neither height nor depth, nor anything else in all creation, will be able to separate us from the love of God that is in Christ Jesus our Lord.

In 1 Corinthians 13:13,

> And now these three remain: faith, hope and love. But the greatest of these is love.

In Joshua 22:5,

> But be very careful to keep the commandment and the law that Moses the servant of the LORD gave you: to love the LORD your God, to walk in obedience to him, to keep his commands, to hold fast to him and to serve him with all your heart and with all your soul.

Action steps

- Express your love and gratitude to the people in your life who have loved you so well.
- Write heartfelt cards for family members to be opened at milestone events in the future.
- Pray to God and let Him know how much you love Him. Tell Him that you trust in His plan for the remainder of your life.

Playlist

"How He Loves," David Crowder[38]
"Beautiful," MercyMe[39]
"Reckless Love," Cory Asbury[40]
"I Could Sing of Your Love Forever," Sonicflood[41]

CHAPTER NINE

Leaving a Legacy

Their children will be mighty in the land; the
generation of the upright will be blessed.

—Psalm 112:2

To leave a legacy is to have fulfilled our God-given purpose
in life and to pass the knowledge and ability to further God's
kingdom to the next generation. Our legacy is evidence of how
we have lived our life. Have we stored up treasures on earth or
stored up treasures in heaven? When we meet Jesus face-to-face,
what will we lay at His feet that He would value?

Rev. Billy Graham said that "the greatest legacy one can
pass on to one's children and grandchildren is not money or
other material things accumulated in one's life, but rather a legacy of character and faith."[42]

A biblical legacy is supported by many pillars: fulfillment
of your God-given purpose, your faith legacy, and a generational legacy.

As Jesus neared His crucifixion, He prayed to God, "I have
brought you glory on earth by finishing the work you gave me to
do" (John 17:4). Jesus knew He was completing God's purpose

for His life, and He was glorifying God while doing so. Similarly, we each have a God-given purpose for our lives. Hebrews 10:36 reminds us, "You need to persevere so that when you have done the will of God, you will receive what he has promised." We are to be intentional in seeking the will of God in our lives and then faithfully complete the work He has given us to do. When we fulfill our God-given purpose, we honor and glorify God.

Our faith legacy revolves around our personal relationship with God. Privately, have we been faithful in prayer? Have we spent time communicating with and listening to God? Would we say that we have built a solid relationship with Jesus Christ? Have we led our family and friends to Jesus Christ? Publicly, do we model love, forgiveness, and generosity? Have we created and fulfilled spiritual goals? Do we truly walk by faith? In the church community, do we attend church? Do we participate in Bible studies? Do we volunteer and serve? Do we support the church financially? Have we led people, nonbelievers, to Jesus Christ?

A generational legacy is a rich family legacy that arises from a godly home. We create a godly home by establishing a firm foundation in our marriages by praying and serving together. We teach our children about Jesus and read them Bible stories. We celebrate Christian holidays and refrain from celebrating secular events that are not in keeping with scripture. We serve the church community together. We teach the children how to pray. We memorize and share our favorite Bible verses. We create plans to pass on generational wealth that will honor God. We ensure our homes are sanctuaries of unconditional love, forgiveness, and generosity. We honor God with spiritual family goals and family traditions.

If you are single, alone, or estranged from your family, consider embracing your church family to fulfill your Biblical legacy. I am so grateful and blessed that Christian adults reached out to me, a neglected young teen, and supported me spiritually.

I have never forgotten their faithfulness, diligence, and patience in answering my questions and softening my fears. The scripture 1 Corinthians 3:10–13 affirms,

> By the grace God has given me, I laid a foundation as a wise builder, and someone else is building on it. But each one should build with care. For no one can lay any foundation other than the one already laid, which is Jesus Christ. If anyone builds on this foundation using gold, silver, costly stones, wood, hay or straw, their work will be shown for what it is, because the Day will bring it to light. It will be revealed with fire, and the fire will test the quality of each person's work.

I am so thankful these Christians laid a foundation in my life, and I pray God finds favor with their work in me, their legacy, that will withstand the fire.

Upon our arrival in heaven, we should be prepared to answer Jesus's question, "What have you done with the time and resources you were given?" We pray we can reply that we took what God gave us and created something more, fulfilling our God-given purpose and providing a legacy that honors Him.

Reflections

In Proverbs 22:1,

> A good name is more desirable than great riches; to be esteemed is better than silver or gold.

In Deuteronomy 6:5–9,

> Love the Lord your God with all your heart and with all your soul and with all your strength. These commandments that I give you today are to be on your hearts. Impress them on your children. Talk about them when you sit at home and when you walk along the road, when you lie down and when you get up. Tie them as symbols on your hands and bind them on your foreheads. Write them on the doorframes of your houses and on your gates.

In Psalm 127:3,

> Children are a heritage from the Lord, offspring a reward from him.

In 1 Timothy 5:8,

> Anyone who does not provide for their relatives, and especially for their own household, has denied the faith and is worse than an unbeliever.

In Proverbs 13:22,

> A good person leaves an inheritance for their children's children, but a sinner's wealth is stored up for the righteous.

In Colossians 3:23–24,

> Whatever you do, work at it with all your heart, as working for the Lord, not for human masters, since you know that you will receive an inheritance from the Lord as a reward. It is the Lord Christ you are serving.

In Psalm 145:3–7,

> Great is the LORD and most worthy of praise; his greatness no one can fathom.
> One generation commends your works to another; they tell of your mighty acts. They speak of the glorious splendor of your majesty—and I will meditate on your wonderful works. They tell of the power of your awesome works—and I will proclaim your great deeds. They celebrate your abundant goodness and joyfully sing of your righteousness.

Action steps

- Start a family Bible to be passed on from generation to generation.
- Record current family traditions or start new family traditions.
- Create a family mission statement to include values and beliefs.
- Develop a plan to transfer tangible assets that will honor and glorify God.

- Write down what you would like your family to say about your legacy at your funeral. Close the gaps now.

Playlist

"Legacy," Nichole Nordeman[43]
"Lifesong," Casting Crowns[44]
"Beautiful Things," Michael Gungor[45]
"I Will Be Here," Steven Curtis Chapman[46]
"The Blessing," Kari Jobe[47]

CHAPTER TEN

Finishing the Race

I have fought the good fight, I have finished
the race, I have kept the faith.

—2 Timothy 4:7

If we have been faithful and prayerful during this study, we have prepared well and nearly completed our tasks for this season, our final season of life on earth. We have surrendered our control to God and chosen to live by faith. We have offered forgiveness and restored relationships. We have prepared to die well while continuing to live well. We have deepened our relationship with the Lord, prayed fervently, and learned to sit in His presence and listen to Him. We have loved our family and friends with a renewed sense of urgency. We have remained active in our church community, modeling how to live well and die well. Finally, we have passed on a legacy that will embrace and comfort our loved ones long after we are gone. Before our journey home, we have completed the spiritual tasks set aside by God, unique to us.

We will be citizens of heaven, hallelujah! Our souls will immediately enter heaven, and later, we will have transformed resurrected bodies. We will be reunited with our family and friends who have gone to heaven before us. We will serve God and praise God. Finally, we will receive our reward in heaven, as Jeremiah 17:10 reminds us, "I the Lord search the heart and examine the mind, to reward each person according to their conduct, according to what their deeds deserve." How exciting to think that we can "have a chat" with the prophets and disciples and to work side by side with those we have only read about! We are victorious over death because of our faith in Jesus Christ.

If you have not yet decided to accept Jesus Christ as your Lord and Savior, today can be your day of salvation. The Bible says,

> If you declare with your mouth, "Jesus is Lord," and believe in your heart that God raised him from the dead, you will be saved. For it is with your heart that you believe and are justified, and it is with your mouth that you profess your faith and are saved. (Romans 10:9–10)

I implore you to consider this, to pray about it, and to choose eternal life today. Then, as our health declines, we can rest knowing we are secure in God's love. He will provide peace, comfort, mercy, and grace for ourselves and our family members. He will drive out fear and worry so that we can truly live our last days with grace in faith.

As we near the end of our race, we ought to continue to perform small acts of kindness for as long as we are able. We can write love letters, give to those in need, share our faith, convey appreciation for visits and calls, be prayer warriors for our church community, share family history and stories, and say, "Goodbye," and, "I love you."

The apostle Paul wrote to the church at Thessalonica to encourage them to remain faithful, despite persecution. "Rejoice always, pray continually, give thanks in all circumstances; for this is God's will for you in Christ Jesus" (1 Thessalonians 5:16–18). Rejoice always means we fix our eyes on Jesus, to be like Jesus, and to praise Him. Pray continually so that we may continue to grow in our relationship with Jesus, to bring new believers to the Christian faith, and to express our gratitude for His continued mercy and love. Give thanks in all circumstances; we will offer our appreciation for the love and care shown to us by our family and friends.

One of the greatest writers of our time, C. S. Lewis, tells us, "It was when I was happiest that I longed most… The sweetest thing in all my life has been the longing…to find the place where all the beauty came from."[48]

I pray that we all have the strength and mercy that only God can bestow so that we may finish our race strong and rejoice together in the presence of God.

Reflections

In John 11:25–26,

> Jesus said to her, "I am the resurrection and the life. The one who believes in me will live, even though they die; and whoever lives by believing in me will never die. Do you believe this?"

In Revelation 21:4,

> He will wipe every tear from their eyes.
> There will be no more death or mourning or
> crying or pain, for the old order of things has
> passed away.

In John 14:1–3,

> Do not let your hearts be troubled. You
> believe in God; believe also in me.
> My Father's house has many rooms; if
> that were not so, would I have told you that
> I am going there to prepare a place for you?
> And if I go and prepare a place for you, I will
> come back and take you to be with me that
> you also may be where I am.

In Psalm 23:4,

> Even though I walk through the darkest
> valley, I will fear no evil, for you are with me;
> your rod and your staff, they comfort me.

In Ecclesiastes 3:1–8,

> There is a time for everything, and a sea-
> son for every activity under the heavens:
> a time to be born and a time to die, a
> time to plant and a time to uproot,
> a time to kill and a time to heal, a time
> to tear down and a time to build,

a time to weep and a time to laugh, a
time to mourn and a time to dance,
a time to scatter stones and a time to
gather them, a time to embrace and a time to
refrain from embracing,
a time to search and a time to give up, a
time to keep and a time to throw away,
a time to tear and a time to mend, a time
to be silent and a time to speak,
a time to love and a time to hate, a time
for war and a time for peace.

In Matthew 5:4,

Blessed are those who mourn, for they
will be comforted.

In John 17:4–5,

I have brought you glory on earth by
finishing the work you gave me to do.
And now, Father, glorify me in your
presence with the glory I had with you before
the world began.

Action steps

- Accept Jesus Christ as your personal Savior. It's never
too late.

Playlist

"Well Done," The Afters[49]
"I Will Rise," Chris Tomlin[50]
"The Commission," Cain[51]
"Weary Traveler," Jordan St. Cyr[52]
"There Will Be a Day," Jeremy Camp[53]
"Nearer My God to Thee," Katherine Jenkins[54]

SUCCESS

He has achieved success who has lived well, laughed often and loved much; who has gained the respect of intelligent men and the love of little children; who has filled his niche and accomplished his task; who has left the world better than he found it, whether by an improved poppy, a perfect poem, or a rescued soul; who has never lacked appreciation of earth's beauty or failed to express it; who has always looked for the best in others and given the best he had; whose life was an inspiration; whose memory a benediction.[55]

—Bessie A. Stanley

ENDNOTES

1. Scriptures are taken from the Holy Bible, New International Version®, NIV®. Copyright © 1973, 1978, 1984, 2011 by Biblica Inc.™ All Bible verses are quoted from the online website Bible Study Tools, Copyright © 2022. All rights reserved. Salem Web Network Proud member of Salem Media Group.
2. Casting Crowns, "Oh My Soul (Official Lyric Video)," Provident Label Group LLC, August 12, 2022, YouTube Music Video, 4:15, https://youtu.be/DjNZf878ISQ.
3. Lauren Daigle, "Trust in You (Lyric Video)," Centricity Music, August 12, 2022, YouTube Music Video, 3:34, https://youtu.be/qv-SXz_exKE.
4. Third Day, "Cry Out to Jesus (Official Video)," Essential Records, August 12, 2022, YouTube Music Video, 4:40, https://youtu.be/JmVxRl5bc4Y.
5. Plumb, "Need You Now (How Many Times) (official lyric video)," Curb Records, August 12, 2022, YouTube Music Video, 4:17, https://youtu.be/9ylnx0NA9X4.
6. Max Lucado, Day 8, Excerpts from *Great Day Every Day*, Originally published under the title *Every Day Deserves a Chance*, TN: Thomas Nelson Publishers, 2007, https://maxlucado.com/30-days-of-thoughts-from-every-day-deserves-a-chance/.
7. Jon Reddick, "God, Turn It Around (Official Lyric Video)," Gotee Records, August 12, 2022, YouTube Music Video, 4:31, https://youtu.be/-Gv8VDqc-os.
8. The Afters, "I Will Fear No More (Official Lyric Video)," Fair Trade Services, August 12, 2022, YouTube Music Video, 3:25, https://youtu.be/wMmmbJlWhtk.
9. Tenth Avenue North, "By Your Side official music video," Reunion Records, August 12, 2022, YouTube Music Video, 4:07, https://youtu.be/iFvQQt6Nbh8.
10. Jeremy Camp, "Out of My Hands (Radio Version/Lyric Video)," Sparrow Records/Capital Christian Music Group, August 14, 2022, YouTube Music Video, 3:49, https://youtu.be/6B_iXPaoTD4.
11. MercyMe, "Even If (Official Lyric Video)," Fair Trade Services, August 12, 2022, YouTube Music Video, 4:17, https://youtu.be/B6fA35Ved-Y.
12. Jonny Diaz, "Breathe" (Official Lyric Video)," Capitol Christian Music Group, August 12, 2022, YouTube Music Video, 3:34, https://youtu.be/hnjeMwxFuBA.

13 Lauren Daigle, "You Say (Lyric Video)," Centricity Music, August 12, 2022, YouTube Music Video, 4:30, https://youtu.be/N8WK9HmF53w.

14 Sidewalk Prophets, "The Words I Would Say," Word Records, August 12, 2022, YouTube Music Video, 3:19, https://youtu.be/8t9u-LOa3OI.

15 Chris Tomlin, "Whom Shall I Fear [God of Angel Armies] (Lyric Video)," Sparrow Records, August 12, 2022, YouTube Music Video, 4:29, https://youtu.be/qOkImV2cJDg.

16 Carrie Underwood, "Great Is Thy Faithfulness featuring CeCe Winans (Official Performance Video)," Capitol Records, August 12, 2022, YouTube Music Video, 4:21, https://youtu.be/NT0HcAr9aeI.

17 Matt Maher, "Hold Us Together," Provident Label Group LLC, August 12, 2022, YouTube Music Video, 3:28, https://youtu.be/gd4dFXMuy-8.

18 Michael W. Smith, "Here I Am to Worship," Reunion Records, August 12, 2022, YouTube Music Video, 4:57, https://youtu.be/O1FVi0QgTq8.

19 No Other Name, "Lead You to the Cross (Official Music Video)," Curb Records, August 12, 2022, YouTube Music Video, 4:39, https://youtu.be/dvp0ksrMPzY.

20 Katy Nichole, "In Jesus Name (God of Possible) (Official Music Video)," Centricity Music, August 12, 2022, YouTube Music Video, 3:50, https://youtu.be/ ihrUIPfvTh8.

21 Martin Luther, ChristianQuotes.info, Pastor Jack Wellman, August 20, 2019.

22 Matt Redman, "Gracefully Broken (Lyric Video) featuring Tasha Cobbs Leonard," Capitol Christian Music Group Inc., August 12, 2022, YouTube Music Video, 5:49, https://youtu.be/ IJNR0lxbIP4.

23 MercyMe, "Homesick (Pseudo Video)," INO Records, August 12, 2022, YouTube Music Video, 3:41, https://youtu.be/PSTCG9qHFy0.

24 Anthem Lights, "It Is Well with My Soul," Wavy Records, August 29, 2022, YouTube Music Video, 3:31, https://youtu.be/jcp6w4zaW7U.

25 Third Day, "Trust in Jesus (Live)," Provident Label Group LLC, a unit of Sony Music Entertainment, August 12, 2022, YouTube Music Video, 3:58, https://youtu.be/fFVeKofo_V4.

26 Rob Moll, *The Art of Dying*, p.55, Illinois: Intervarsity Press, 2010.

27 Stephen Kiernan, *Last Rights: Rescuing the End of Life from the Medical System*, p. 12, New York: St. Martin's Press, 2006.

28 Casting Crowns, "Who Am I (Official Lyric Video)," Be Essential Songs (BMI)/My Refuge Music (BMI), August 12, 2022, YouTube Music Video, 5:34, https://youtu.be/qOkImV2cJDg.

29 Natalie Grant, "In Christ Alone," Curb Records Inc., August 12, 2022, YouTube Music Video, 5:33, https://youtu.be/RrsgQCywgxI.

30 Michael W. Smith, "Sovereign Over Us (Lyric Video)," Sparrow Records, August 12, 2022, YouTube Music Video, 5:55, https://youtu.be/Lay-r2g52SQ.

31 MercyMe, "I Can Only Imagine (Video)," INO Records, August 12, 2022, YouTube Music Video, 4:07, https://youtu.be/ N_lrrq_opng.

32 Jordan St. Cyr, "Fires (Lyric Video)," Collide Records, August 12, 2022, YouTube Music Video, 3:51, https://youtu.be/H-ggZd-SmSs.

33 Ira Byock, *The Four Things That Matter Most*, p.3, New York: Atria Books, 2014.

34 Matthew West, "Forgiveness (Lyric Video)," Sparrow Records, August 12, 2022, YouTube Music Video, 3:49, https://youtu.be/oIbCpy0CQEo.

35 Crowder, "Forgiven (Lyric Video)," Sparrow Records, August 12, 2022, YouTube Music Video, 3:56, https://youtu.be/uUiwA1JNDig.

36 Gabriel Henrique, "Oh Happy Day," August 12, 2022, YouTube Music Video, 4:00, https://youtu.be/QmxtdvfA1OE.

37 TobyMac, "Forgiveness [Lyrics] featuring Lecrae," ForeFront Records, August 12, 2022, YouTube Music Video, 4:15, https://youtu.be/xfkhqpl81NA.

38 David Crowder*Band, "How He Loves Us (Official Music Video)", Essential Records, August 12, 2022, YouTube Music Video, 4:08, https://youtu.be/TCunuL58odQ.

39 MercyMe, "Beautiful (Live-Video)," INO Records, August 12, 2022, YouTube Music Video, 4:28, https://youtu.be/1vh7-RSPuAA.

40 Cory Asbury, "Reckless Love (Official Lyric Video)," Bethel Music, August 12, 2022, YouTube Music Video, 5:33, https://youtu.be/Sc6SSHuZvQE.

41 Sonic Flood, "I Could Sing of Your Love Forever," Gotee Records, August 12, 2022, YouTube Music Video, 4:25, https://youtu.be/t4Lme31F4is.

42 Billy Graham Quotes. BrainyQuote.com, BrainyMedia Inc, 2022. https://www.brainyquote.com/quotes/billy_graham_626354, accessed August 28, 2022.

43 Nichole Nordeman, "Legacy," Sparrow Records, August 12, 2022, YouTube Music Video, 3:46, https://youtu.be/PnHl_sF_54A.

44 Casting Crowns, "Lifesong (Official Lyric Video)," Be Essential Songs (BMI)/ My Refuge Music (BMI), August 12, 2022, YouTube Music Video, 5:21, https://youtu.be/oEhlwljvOq0.

45 Gungor, "Beautiful Things," Brash Music, August 12, 2022, YouTube Music Video, 5:11, https://youtu.be/gpOPkzplHRw.

46 Steven Curtis Chapman, "I Will Be Here," Sparrow Records, August 12, 2022, YouTube Music Video, 4:13, https://youtu.be/JJZYVYsCnoU.

47 Kari Jobe, Cody Carnes, Elevation Worship, "The Blessing (Live) [Official Lyric Video]," Elevation Worship Records, August 12, 2022, YouTube Music Video, 8:36, https://youtu.be/YtpgKKqgfEA.

48 C. S. Lewis, Till We Have Faces (1956, 2006), p. 52-53. HarperCollins Publishers Inc., NY, NY accessed 080622 on Books Vooks (online platform)

49 The Afters, "Well Done (Official Lyric Video)," Epic Records, August 12, 2022, YouTube Music Video, 4:37, https://youtu.be/X29hPMgKUyM.

50 Chris Tomlin, "I Will Rise," Sparrow Records, August 12, 2022, YouTube Music Video, 5:00, https://youtu.be/l6paJbntGpU.

51 CAIN, "The Commission (Official Lyric Video)," Provident Label Group LLC, a division of Sony Music Entertainment, August 12, 2022, YouTube Music Video, 3:16, https://youtu.be/XkJniP87XdQ.

52 Jordan St. Cyr, "Weary Traveler (Official Music Video)," Collide Records, August 12, 2022, YouTube Music Video, 4:00, https://youtu.be/io8GX4zMemg.

53 Jeremy Camp, "There Will Be a Day (Lyric Video)," Capitol Christian Music Group, August 12, 2022, YouTube Music Video, 4:40, https://youtu.be/CPKyTY71iRM.

54 Katherine Jenkins, "Nearer My God to Thee," Universal Music Operations Limited, August 12, 2022, YouTube Music Video, 5:15, https://youtu.be/jlOljwm_K5s.

55 Bessie A. Stanley, *Success*, Massachusetts: Brown Book Magazine, 1904.

ABOUT THE AUTHOR

Maureen Sobolewski is terminally ill and writes with a heart for those in the same season of life. She is happiest showering her family with love and beautiful memories while living in faith and obedience to God. She is married to her best friend, Brad, and they are incredibly blessed with two sons, two daughters-in-law, five grandchildren, and a grandbaby on the way—and an old German shepherd. Having lived in Michigan, Tennessee, Florida, and Georgia, the family currently resides in the picturesque state of Colorado.